GW01046539

W. B. YEATS

THE WILD SWANS AT COOLE (1919)

A FACSIMILE EDITION

WITH AN INTRODUCTION AND NOTES
BY
GEORGE BORNSTEIN

SCRIBNER
NEW YORK LONDON TORONTO SYDNEY NEW DELHI

SCRIBNER
An Imprint of Simon & Schuster, Inc.
1230 Avenue of the Americas
New York, NY 10020

This book is a work of fiction. Any references to historical events, real people, or real places are used fictitiously. Other names, characters, places, and events are products of the author's imagination, and any resemblance to actual events or places or persons, living or dead, is entirely coincidental.

First Scribner trade paperback edition March 2017

Interior design by Erich Hobbing

Manufactured in the United States of America

1 3 5 7 9 10 8 6 4 2

Library of Congress Cataloging-in-Publication Data is available.

ISBN 978-1-5011-0604-0
ISBN 978-1-5011-0605-7 (ebook)

CONTENTS

PREFACE

This edition offers a facsimile of the expanded first London edition of *The Wild Swans at Coole*, first published in London by Macmillan on March 11, 1919. It was a considerable expansion of the earlier 1917 volume published in Ireland by the Cuala Press on November 17, 1917. The copy used is from my own personal library, except for the cover and spine design, which, because of greater clarity, come from the identical second printing in the Special Collections Library of the University of Michigan in Ann Arbor. The present edition adds an introduction tracing the assembly and design of the 1919 volume as well as annotations to that edition, including editorial notes on the poems.

I am grateful to the late Richard J. Finneran of the University of Tennessee for suggesting this project some years ago, and to Ashley Gilliam at Scribner for support in following it through. I am also grateful to the splendid librarians at the University of Michigan, and particularly to the head of Special Collections, Martha O'Hara Conway. Rebecca Huffman served as capable and cheerful research assistant.

This edition is dedicated to my daughter, Rebecca York Bornstein, and to Alex Roy on the occasion of their marriage.

INTRODUCTION TO YEATS'S *THE WILD SWANS AT COOLE*

As the great critic Hugh Kenner pointed out some time ago, Yeats not only wrote poems but also arranged them into carefully wrought books. "The place to look for light on any poem is in the adjacent poems," argued Kenner. "And the unit in which to inspect and discuss his development is not the poem or sequence of poems but the volume."[1] Yeats's drafts and notebooks contain numerous alternate arrangements of the poems for each of his individual volumes and for his collected ones as well. A lifelong reviser, he went through draft after draft when working on a poem, and continued the process even after first publication. This series of Scribner paperback facsimiles thus gives readers a sense of the state of the texts in their first important gathering into individual volumes. In Yeats's case, that sense involves not only verbal reproduction but also layout and design. From the much-reprinted 1895 *Poems* onward, Yeats gained enough control to incorporate those latter features into his

1 Hugh Kenner, "The Sacred Book of the Arts," in his *Gnomon* (New York: Ivan Obolensky, 1958), and often reprinted.

books, as his admired William Blake had done before him. For the first commercial Macmillan edition of *The Wild Swans at Coole* he worked with his friend and favorite designer, T. Sturge Moore. This introduction sketches the assembling and design of that crucial 1919 volume.

The Wild Swans at Coole appeared in two different book formats before 1920. The earlier and shorter volume, *The Wild Swans at Coole: Other Verses and a Play in Verse* (1917), contained seventeen lyrics, including the seven-part "Upon a Dying Lady," along with the Noh-like Cuchulain play *At the Hawk's Well*. That version was published by Cuala Press, a fine-arts private press operated chiefly by Yeats's sister Lolly that featured handcrafting and small print runs (in this case, only four hundred copies). Two years later, Macmillan published the revised and expanded volume, deleting the play and adding sixteen additional poems to double the size of the collection and nearly quadruple the print run. In the order in which they appear in the volume, the new poems sprang from the death of aviator Major Robert Gregory in World War I; Yeats's marriage to Georgie Hyde-Lees; his rocky relations with Maud Gonne and her daughter, Iseult; and the resultant emergence of material related to Yeats's book of esoteric philosophy *A Vision* (1925; revised 1937). It is the second, longer version of *The Wild Swans at Coole* that is reproduced here. Unlike the more defeatist tone of the 1917 volume, the revised one shows a progress from the ambiguous opening title poem through immersion in life and death to the final imaginative success of "The Double Vision of Michael Robartes" at the end.

That development starts with the evolution of the title poem itself. Copious manuscript drafts display a dark tone of death and imaginative defeat. The first one sketches natural decline with its mention of low water, brown leaves, and sunset: "The water in the lake is low / The leaves turn brown / And [I] go out toward sun set / To number the swans. . . . / The autumn rains have not begun." The entire poem, dated October 1916 and first published in *The Little Review* in June 1917, sounds a mournful, elegiac note ending with an invocation of autumn and a lack of rain. But when he came to collect the poem in book form, Yeats made one of his most brilliant revisions, raising the work to allow at least the possibility of a more positive outcome befitting the title poem of a new poetic volume, his first after turning fifty. He did that by repositioning the third stanza to come last of the five. The magazine version had ended by contrasting the vitality of the swans to the implicit waning of the poet's powers in old age:

> Their hearts have not grown old;
> Passion or conquest, wander where they will,
> Attend upon them still.

In contrast to the swans, the speaker's heart has grown old, and passion and conquest no longer await him. The final lines in both book versions instead hold open a possibility of a more positive ending, together with an ambiguity about what the poet will "awake" to:

> By what lake's edge or pool
> Delight men's eyes when I awake some day
> To find they have flown away.

Does he awake to the natural world to find the swans gone, or rather a spiritual world after death? The poem exhibits a typical Yeatsian fondness for what we might call "anticlosure closure," an ending that leaves the door open for more verse to follow.

Picking up on the opening poem, set on the estate of Yeats's patron, friend, and collaborator Lady Gregory, Yeats followed it in the 1919 volume with two new poems on the death of her son, Robert, an aviator in World War I. That premature passing robbed the Coole estate of its obvious heir and thus intensified the melancholy of "The Wild Swans at Coole" about the diminishing effects of time. If, as Marjorie Perloff has suggested, the first poem marks Yeats's first work with a speaker closely identified with Yeats himself planted in a specific landscape and interacting with it, "In Memory of Major Robert Gregory" shows its expansion into a full-blown Greater Romantic Lyric. Such poems, like Wordsworth's "Tintern Abbey" and Coleridge's "The Eolian Harp," among many others, or even Keats's "Ode on a Grecian Urn," tend to divide into three or sometimes four parts. In the first, the speaker describes a specific landscape or object; in the second, he or she enters into an imaginative vision inspired by it; and in the third, the speaker reemerges with new insight or knowledge. The mature Yeats constructed a number of such poems, including "The Tower" part II and "Meditations in Time of Civil War" part XII.

"In Memory of Major Robert Gregory," one of the great poems of Yeats's maturity, is written in octaves and follows the three-part Romantic pattern. It begins with a description of Yeats and his wife as "almost settled" in their newly acquired tower, Thoor Ballylee, near Coole, their summer home for the coming decade. In the vision section, the poet first calls up three dead figures with whom he had been close—the learned poet Lionel Johnson, the dramatist John M. Synge (author of *The Playboy of the Western World*), and Yeats's maternal uncle George Pollexfen, well-versed in both horsemanship and astrology. He then devotes six stanzas to Major Robert Gregory, who combines their virtues into a sort of Renaissance ideal like that of Sir Philip Sidney, "soldier, scholar, horseman he," as well as artist and craftsman. The poet emerges from his imaginings of Gregory in the final stanza, where he reveals that his original plan had been to call up others, but Gregory "took all my heart for speech." Biographical events intrude here even more than in most places for Yeats, who added the eighth stanza (on horsemanship) at the request of Gregory's widow.

And, of course, Gregory is the unnamed "Irish Airman" of the short following poem.

After two lyrics on old age from the original volume, Yeats then inserted a new group on love, the first to his wife as Sheba to his Solomon, and several stemming from his brief infatuation with Maud Gonne's daughter, Iseult. Another short group culminates in "The Fisherman," an important turning point in the volume and in Yeats's career as a whole. Writing in short quatrains using strong, down-to-earth language, Yeats bids farewell to his earlier work, not only from the 1890s but from his more recent strife in Irish politics and drama, both of which feature "The beating down of the wise / And great Art beaten down." Instead, he nominates for audience a solitary fisherman dressed in "grey Connemara clothes" (which in fact had to be imported from Scotland) and hopes to write him a poem "as cold / And passionate as the dawn." That phrase, "cold and passionate," nicely combines what Yeats called "antinomies," or opposites, in place of the usual conception of passion as warm. He now scorns the rhetoric of debate and mass audiences for the solitary figure of the West of Ireland fisherman, in line with his own adage that out of the quarrel with others comes rhetoric, but out of the quarrel with oneself poetry.

There follows a suite of eight poems beginning and ending with the short lyrics "Memory" and "Presences." They both reprise Yeats's decades-long devotion to Maud Gonne, and as they progress they suggest saying good-bye to her as the poet did to the wild swans in the opening lyric. One of the most substantial works is the dialogue poem "The People," in which the speaker flirts with an urge to quit "the daily spite of this unmannerly town" for more solitary pleasures like those of the writer in Italian Renaissance courts such as Ferrara or Urbino. The beloved replies in line with her own nationalist experience that even in disrepute she had never "complained of the people." To which he ripostes that in contrast to her single-minded dedication, his own analytical mind displays more division. Nevertheless, in the last line he "sink[s] my head abashed." Like "Her Praise," "His Phoenix" sings the past glory of the beloved in the face of her present aging. The last major poem, "Broken Dreams," again turns on the speaker's reminiscence of the beloved's past beauty, yet at the end he censures himself for spending the entire day lost in "Vague memories, nothing but memories." After two shorter poems still about the beloved, the volume moves on to three short poems, concluding with "On Being Asked for a War Poem." Instead of their present title the five lines were called "A Reason for Keeping Silent" upon publication in Edith Wharton's anthology *The Book of the Homeless* (1916), and the second line began not with the more elevated "A poet's mouth be silent" but with the more blunt "We poets keep our mouths shut," as it did in the singular in both the 1917 and 1919 volumes of *Wild Swans*. This section of the volume concludes with two elegies, neither of them for anyone killed in World War I or the Easter Rising. Rather, each commemorates a person whom Yeats knew personally—first his maternal grandfather, Alfred Pollexfen, and then the Victorian actress Mabel Beardsley, older sister of Yeats's friend the Art Nouveau artist and illustrator Aubrey Beardsley. Alfred Pollexfen responded to the call of home after his years working in London, while Mabel Beardsley, in her struggle with cancer, embodied the courage in the face of death that Yeats always admired.

The poem "Ego Dominus Tuus," which means "I am your Lord," marks the onset of the volume's final phase. Yeats cast the poem as a dialogue between Hic (Latin for "this one") and Ille (Latin for "that one"), although Ille's views come so close to Yeats's own that his mercurial sometime secretary Ezra Pound dubbed it a dialogue between Hic and Willie. The two form another pair of opposites, with Hic representing what Yeats would call the primary or objective man and Ille the secondary or subjective one. Hic believes that the poet creates a self-portrait in his work, while Ille believes that the portrait in the work represents the opposite of the poet, as with Dante and Keats. Mocked by Guido Cavalcanti for his "lecherous life," Dante created in his work the image of an austere quester, while Keats made "luxuriant song" in opposition to the poem's notorious image of him as a schoolboy with "nose pressed to a sweet-shop window." Ille seeks just such an antinomial "image," one of his opposite or, as the poem dubs it, his "anti-self." Yeats published the dialogue in 1917, shortly after both Maud Gonne and her daughter, Iseult, turned down his marriage proposals.

Out of Yeats's subsequent marriage to Georgie Hyde-Lees would come the material published in *A Vision*, which the Yeatses began to work out almost immediately, at the time of the remaining poems in *The Wild Swans at Coole*. Published first in 1925 and then in highly revised form in 1937, *A Vision* systematized the abstruse material growing out of Georgie's "automatic writing," which purported to come from various "instructors." A complicated work of esoteric philosophy, the book emphasized two main aspects utilized in the poetry, one psychological and the other historical, both represented by interlocking gyres. The psychological section "The Phases of the Moon" divided human life into twenty-eight categories according to lunar phases, with no human life possible at the extremes of phases 1 or 15. Similar interlocking gyres represented a cyclic view of human history expounded in the "Dove or Swan" section, a subtitle balancing the dove of the annunciation with Mary fostering the Christian civilization that succeeded the Classical one begun by the story of Leda. Some readers find the resultant systems insightful, while others tend to agree with Ezra Pound (always more skeptical of others' systems than of his own) that it was "very very bughouse."

The remaining half dozen poems in the volume

all grow out of the *Vision* system. Yeats came to be uncertain of their poetic as opposed to esoteric value and confessed in a 1922 note that "to some extent I wrote these poems as a text for exposition." The longest of them, "The Phases of the Moon," dramatizes another dialogue between Robartes and Aherne taking place on the roadside at night by a tower very like Yeats's own with a figure inside it very like Yeats himself. The poem associates that Yeatsian figure with Shelley's Prince Athanase and Milton's Il Penseroso, who also studied alone in towers, before versifying accounts of the twenty-eight phases. The poem ends as the scene does, with the light in the tower window being put out. After the semicomic "The Cat and the Moon," with its borrowing of the name of Maud Gonne's cat, Minnaloushe, the representative types of the last three phases—Saint, Hunchback, and Fool—sing intervening poems before the strong conclusion of the volume in "The Double Vision of Michael Robartes."

As so often with Yeats's books, the final poem makes an interesting contrast with the opening one. In the title poem at the beginning, the poet had felt his powers in decline, as opposed to the continued natural vitality of the swans. By the end, though, he has restored his visionary capacity and displays it through a vision ascribed once more to Michael Robartes. On the rock of Cashel, one of Ireland's most famous ruined ecclesiastical sites, the poet sees a vision of a Sphinx and a Buddha, between which a girl dances. He does so at the fifteenth phase of the moon, when human life becomes impossible. The Sphinx seems to represent intellect and the Buddha love, with the girl having "outdanced thought" to achieve that "body perfection" that Yeats always admired, as at the famous ending of "Among School Children." The speaker sees the scene in his "mind's eye," a phrase from Shakespeare's *Hamlet* that Yeats uses elsewhere to represent vision, just as he here also invokes Blakean "minute particulars." In part three he emerges from that vision and returns to his normal self in "Cormac's ruined house," the ruined Romanesque chapel constructed in the twelfth century by Cormac MacCarthy, king of Munster. It is yet another instance of Yeats's penchant for closure that resists closure, as he would label his next volume *Michael Robartes and the Dancer.*

Besides organizing and ordering his individual poems in thematic rather than chronological order for *The Wild Swans at Coole*, Yeats paid attention to layout and design, as he customarily did from 1895 onward. For cover design he turned to his friend T. Sturge Moore, an English writer and artist who was also his favorite book designer. Moore had already devised some covers for Yeats's books, and would design more. For *Wild Swans* he disregarded Yeats's suggestions of adapting the cover of the prose volume *Per Amica Silentia Lunae* (published the previous year) but with a different emblem and instead produced a new design continuing the interaction of circles and rectangles on the cover of that earlier book. Stamped in gold on a blue background, the new cover featured a swan in a circle at the top looking down and the top half of a swan at the bottom, both in flight. They thus reinforced the prominence of the title poem of the book, and at the same time enacted one of Yeats's favorite dichotomies of up/down, or "as above, so below." The interior layout stressed the formal integrity of each poem, beginning each on a new page, even if that required an unusual amount of white space.

Surprisingly to a modern reader, this first major volume of Yeats's maturity drew mixed notice from reviewers. Some of them longed for the sentiments and magic of the earlier poetry rather than this new, more grounded and difficult Yeats. "Where are all the fire and magic of those early years?" asked Charles Hanson Towne in *The Bookman*, yet he also lamented the refusal to write poetry about World War I. The better-known critic John Middleton Murry blasted *The Wild Swans at Coole* as showing Yeats "downcast and defeated from the great quest of poetry" and detected a "disaster in the poet's development." At the other and more positive end of the scale, the poet Marianne Moore expressed in *Poetry: A Magazine of Verse* her "reverence to a poet who, after having written poetry for many years, can still be read with the same critical alertness." Yet Katharine Tynan, Yeats's former fellow member of Young Ireland who had retreated into Catholic orthodoxy, could still praise the beauty of the title poem but object strongly to the intrusion of Yeats's new and idiosyncratic esotericism, calling down "a plague upon what has led him to those fountains of a fantastic and meddling philosophy." In London, the *Times Literary Supplement* complained that Yeats "seems to be living on memories," yet praised "the beauty of his poetry" and concluded that "we can only listen and be grateful." Across the ocean, the *New York Times* made a rare mention of the beauty of the physical book and its cover "of exquisite simplicity designed by Mr. Sturge Moore" and noted that "sadness" pervades the volume. While many reviews labeled "The Wild Swans at Coole" and "In Memory of Major Robert Gregory" major poems, the *Times* also noted that some of the minor poems, such as "His Phoenix" or "Men Improve with the Years," "would make the fame of a lesser poet." The overall impression was that Yeats was in transition, and some readers liked the changes more than others. The present book enables readers to judge for themselves the first major volume of Yeats's mature modernism.

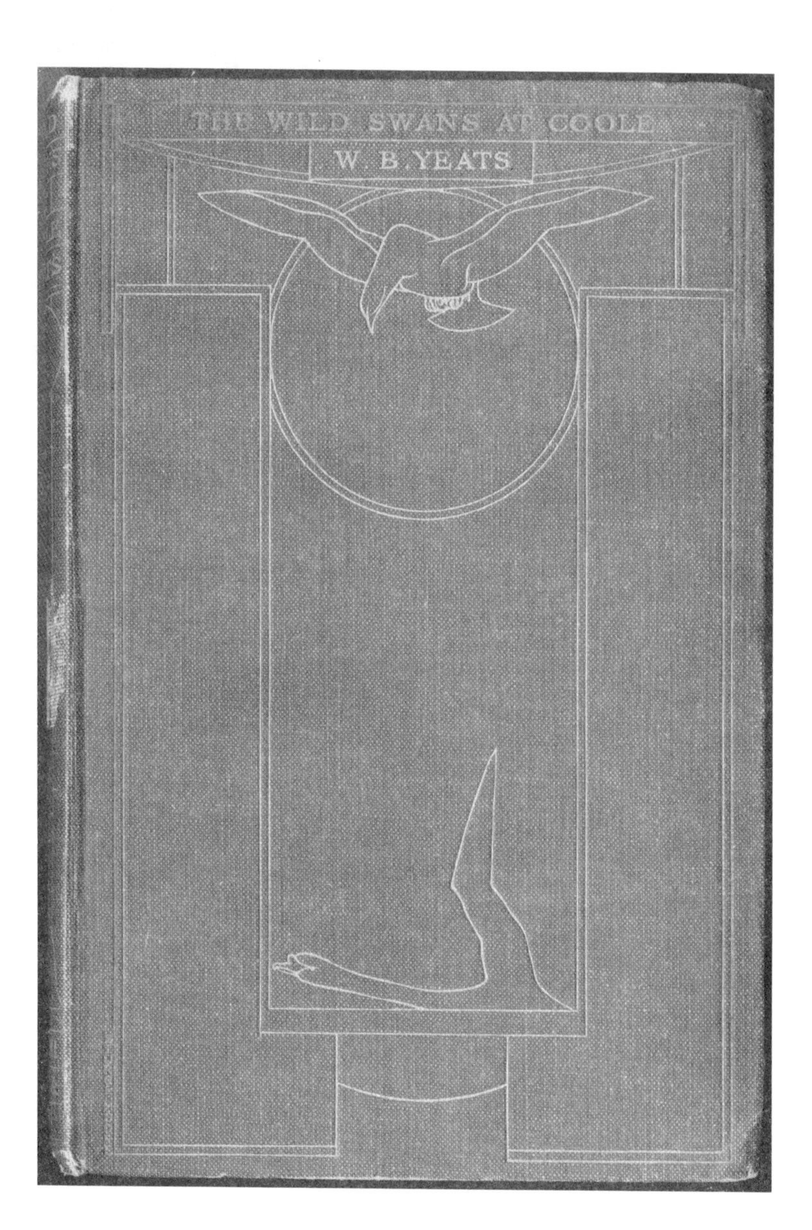
THE WILD SWANS AT COOLE
W. B. YEATS

THE WILD SWANS AT COOLE

MACMILLAN AND CO., Limited
LONDON · BOMBAY · CALCUTTA · MADRAS
MELBOURNE

THE MACMILLAN COMPANY
NEW YORK · BOSTON · CHICAGO
DALLAS · SAN FRANCISCO

THE MACMILLAN CO. OF CANADA, Ltd.
TORONTO

THE WILD SWANS AT COOLE

BY

W. B. YEATS

MACMILLAN AND CO., LIMITED
ST. MARTIN'S STREET, LONDON
1919

PREFACE

THIS book is, in part, a reprint of *The Wild Swans at Coole*, printed a year ago on my sister's hand-press at Dundrum, Co. Dublin. I have not, however, reprinted a play which may be a part of a book of new plays suggested by the dance plays of Japan, and I have added a number of new poems. Michael Robartes and John Aherne, whose names occur in one or other of these, are characters in some stories I wrote years ago, who have once again become a part of the phantasmagoria through which I can alone express my convictions about the world. I have the fancy that I read the name John Aherne among those of men prosecuted for making a disturbance at the first production of "The Play Boy" which may account for his animosity to myself.

W. B. Y.

BALLYLEE, CO. GALWAY,
September 1918.

CONTENTS

CONTENTS

THE WILD SWANS AT COOLE

THE trees are in their autumn beauty,
The woodland paths are dry,
Under the October twilight the water
Mirrors a still sky;
Upon the brimming water among the
stones
Are nine and fifty swans.

The nineteenth Autumn has come
upon me
Since I first made my count;
I saw, before I had well finished,
All suddenly mount
And scatter wheeling in great broken
rings
Upon their clamorous wings.

I have looked upon those brilliant
creatures,
And now my heart is sore.
All's changed since I, hearing at twi-
light,
The first time on this shore,
The bell-beat of their wings above my
head,
Trod with a lighter tread.

Unwearied still, lover by lover,
They paddle in the cold,
Companionable streams or climb the
air ;
Their hearts have not grown old ;
Passion or conquest, wander where
they will,
Attend upon them still.

But now they drift on the still
water
Mysterious, beautiful ;

Among what rushes will they build,
By what lake's edge or pool
Delight men's eyes when I awake
some day
To find they have flown away ?

IN MEMORY OF MAJOR ROBERT GREGORY

1

Now that we're almost settled in our
house
I'll name the friends that cannot sup
with us
Beside a fire of turf in th' ancient
tower,
And having talked to some late
hour
Climb up the narrow winding stair to
bed :
Discoverers of forgotten truth
Or mere companions of my youth,
All, all are in my thoughts to-night
being dead.

2

Always we'd have the new friend meet
the old
And we are hurt if either friend seem
cold,
And there is salt to lengthen out the
smart
In the affections of our heart,
And quarrels are blown up upon that
head ;
But not a friend that I would bring
This night can set us quarrelling,
For all that come into my mind are
dead.

3

Lionel Johnson comes the first to mind,
That loved his learning better than
mankind,
Though courteous to the worst ; much
falling he
Brooded upon sanctity

Till all his Greek and Latin learning seemed
A long blast upon the horn that brought
A little nearer to his thought
A measureless consummation that he dreamed.

4

And that enquiring man John Synge comes next
That dying chose the living world for text
And never could have rested in the tomb
But that, long travelling, he had come
Towards nightfall upon certain set apart
In a most desolate stony place,
Towards nightfall upon a race
Passionate and simple like his heart.

5

And then I think of old George
Pollexfen,
In muscular youth well known to
Mayo men
For horsemanship at meets or at race-
courses,
That could have shown how purebred
horses
And solid men, for all their passion, live
But as the outrageous stars incline
By opposition, square and trine;
Having grown sluggish and contem-
plative.

6

They were my close companions many
a year,
A portion of my mind and life, as it
were,
And now their breathless faces seem
to look

Out of some old picture-book;
I am accustomed to their lack of
breath,
But not that my dear friend's dear son,
Our Sidney and our perfect man,
Could share in that discourtesy of
death.

7

For all things the delighted eye now
sees
Were loved by him; the old storm-
broken trees
That cast their shadows upon road
and bridge;
The tower set on the stream's edge;
The ford where drinking cattle make
a stir
Nightly, and startled by that sound
The water-hen must change her
ground;
He might have been your heartiest
welcomer.

8

When with the Galway foxhounds he
would ride
From Castle Taylor to the Rox-
borough side
Or Esserkelly plain, few kept his
pace ;
At Mooneen he had leaped a place
So perilous that half the astonished
meet
Had shut their eyes, and where
was it
He rode a race without a bit ?
And yet his mind outran the horses'
feet.

9

We dreamed that a great painter had
been born
To cold Clare rock and Galway rock
and thorn,

To that stern colour and that delicate
line
That are our secret discipline
Wherein the gazing heart doubles her
might.
Soldier, scholar, horseman, he,
And yet he had the intensity
To have published all to be a world's
delight.

10

What other could so well have coun-
selled us
In all lovely intricacies of a house
As he that practised or that under-
stood
All work in metal or in wood,
In moulded plaster or in carven stone ?
Soldier, scholar, horseman, he,
And all he did done perfectly
As though he had but that one trade
alone.

11

Some burn damp fagots, others may consume
The entire combustible world in one small room
As though dried straw, and if we turn about
The bare chimney is gone black out
Because the work had finished in that flare.
Soldier, scholar, horseman, he,
As 'twere all life's epitome.
What made us dream that he could comb grey hair?

12

I had thought, seeing how bitter is that wind
That shakes the shutter, to have brought to mind

All those that manhood tried, or child-
hood loved
Or boyish intellect approved,
With some appropriate commentary
on each ;
Until imagination brought
A fitter welcome ; but a thought
Of that late death took all my heart
for speech.

AN IRISH AIRMAN FORESEES HIS DEATH

I KNOW that I shall meet my fate
Somewhere among the clouds above;
Those that I fight I do not hate,
Those that I guard I do not love;
My country is Kiltartan Cross,
My countrymen Kiltartan's poor,
No likely end could bring them loss
Or leave them happier than before.
Nor law, nor duty bade me fight,
Nor public man, nor angry crowds,
A lonely impulse of delight
Drove to this tumult in the clouds;
I balanced all, brought all to mind,
The years to come seemed waste of
breath,
A waste of breath the years behind
In balance with this life, this death.

MEN IMPROVE WITH THE YEARS

I AM worn out with dreams;
A weather-worn, marble triton
Among the streams;
And all day long I look
Upon this lady's beauty
As though I had found in book
A pictured beauty,
Pleased to have filled the eyes
Or the discerning ears,
Delighted to be but wise,
For men improve with the years;
And yet and yet
Is this my dream, or the truth?
O would that we had met
When I had my burning youth;
But I grow old among dreams,
A weather-worn, marble triton
Among the streams.

THE COLLAR-BONE OF A HARE

Would I could cast a sail on the water
Where many a king has gone
And many a king's daughter,
And alight at the comely trees and the
lawn,
The playing upon pipes and the dan-
cing,
And learn that the best thing is
To change my loves while dancing
And pay but a kiss for a kiss.

I would find by the edge of that water
The collar-bone of a hare
Worn thin by the lapping of water,
And pierce it through with a gimlet
and stare

16 COLLAR-BONE OF A HARE

At the old bitter world where they
  marry in churches,
And laugh over the untroubled water
At all who marry in churches,
Through the white thin bone of a hare.

UNDER THE ROUND TOWER

'ALTHOUGH I'd lie lapped up in linen
A deal I'd sweat and little earn
If I should live as live the neighbours,'
Cried the beggar, Billy Byrne;
'Stretch bones till the daylight come
On great-grandfather's battered tomb.'

Upon a grey old battered tombstone
In Glendalough beside the stream,
Where the O'Byrnes and Byrnes are
buried,
He stretched his bones and fell in a
dream
Of sun and moon that a good hour
Bellowed and pranced in the round
tower;

Of golden king and silver lady,
Bellowing up and bellowing round,
Till toes mastered a sweet measure,
Mouth mastered a sweet sound,
Prancing round and prancing up
Until they pranced upon the top.

That golden king and that wild lady
Sang till stars began to fade,
Hands gripped in hands, toes close
together,
Hair spread on the wind they made ;
That lady and that golden king
Could like a brace of blackbirds sing.

' It's certain that my luck is broken,'
That rambling jailbird Billy said ;
' Before nightfall I'll pick a pocket
And snug it in a feather-bed,
I cannot find the peace of home
On great-grandfather's battered tomb.'

SOLOMON TO SHEBA

SANG Solomon to Sheba,
And kissed her dusky face,
'All day long from mid-day
We have talked in the one place,
All day long from shadowless noon
We have gone round and round
In the narrow theme of love
Like an old horse in a pound.'

To Solomon sang Sheba,
Planted on his knees,
'If you had broached a matter
That might the learned please,
You had before the sun had thrown
Our shadows on the ground
Discovered that my thoughts, not it,
Are but a narrow pound.'

Sang Solomon to Sheba,
And kissed her Arab eyes,
'There's not a man or woman
Born under the skies
Dare match in learning with us two,
And all day long we have found
There's not a thing but love can make
The world a narrow pound.'

THE LIVING BEAUTY

I'll say and maybe dream I have
drawn content—
Seeing that time has frozen up the
blood,
The wick of youth being burned and
the oil spent—
From beauty that is cast out of a
mould
In bronze, or that in dazzling marble
appears,
Appears, and when we have gone is
gone again,
Being more indifferent to our solitude
Than 'twere an apparition. O heart,
we are old,
The living beauty is for younger men,
We cannot pay its tribute of wild tears.

A SONG

I THOUGHT no more was needed
Youth to prolong
Than dumb-bell and foil
To keep the body young.
Oh, who could have foretold
That the heart grows old ?

Though I have many words,
What woman's satisfied,
I am no longer faint
Because at her side ?
Oh, who could have foretold
That the heart grows old ?

I have not lost desire
But the heart that I had,
I thought 'twould burn my body
Laid on the death-bed.
But who could have foretold
That the heart grows old ?

TO A YOUNG BEAUTY

DEAR fellow-artist, why so free
With every sort of company,
With every Jack and Jill?
Choose your companions from the best;
Who draws a bucket with the rest
Soon topples down the hill.

You may, that mirror for a school,
Be passionate, not bountiful
As common beauties may,
Who were not born to keep in trim
With old Ezekiel's cherubim
But those of Beaujolet.

I know what wages beauty gives,
How hard a life her servant lives,
Yet praise the winters gone;
There is not a fool can call me friend,
And I may dine at journey's end
With Landor and with Donne.

TO A YOUNG GIRL

My dear, my dear, I know
More than another
What makes your heart beat so;
Not even your own mother
Can know it as I know,
Who broke my heart for her
When the wild thought,
That she denies
And has forgot,
Set all her blood astir
And glittered in her eyes.

THE SCHOLARS

BALD heads forgetful of their sins,
Old, learned, respectable bald heads
Edit and annotate the lines
That young men, tossing on their beds,
Rhymed out in love's despair
To flatter beauty's ignorant ear.

They'll cough in the ink to the world's
end;
Wear out the carpet with their shoes
Earning respect; have no strange
friend;
If they have sinned nobody knows.
Lord, what would they say
Should their Catullus walk that way?

TOM O'ROUGHLEY

'THOUGH logic choppers rule the town,
And every man and maid and boy
Has marked a distant object down,
An aimless joy is a pure joy,'
Or so did Tom O'Roughley say
That saw the surges running by,
'And wisdom is a butterfly
And not a gloomy bird of prey.

'If little planned is little sinned
But little need the grave distress.
What's dying but a second wind?
How but in zig-zag wantonness
Could trumpeter Michael be so brave?'
Or something of that sort he said,
'And if my dearest friend were dead
I'd dance a measure on his grave.'

THE SAD SHEPHERD

SHEPHERD

THAT cry's from the first cuckoo of the year.
I wished before it ceased.

GOATHERD

Nor bird nor beast
Could make me wish for anything this day,
Being old, but that the old alone might die,
And that would be against God's Providence.
Let the young wish. But what has brought you here?
Never until this moment have we met

Where my goats browse on the scarce
grass or leap
From stone to stone.

SHEPHERD

I am looking for strayed sheep;
Something has troubled me and in
my trouble
I let them stray. I thought of rhyme
alone,
For rhyme can beat a measure out
of trouble
And make the daylight sweet once
more; but when
I had driven every rhyme into its
place
The sheep had gone from theirs.

GOATHERD

I know right well
What turned so good a shepherd from
his charge.

SHEPHERD

He that was best in every country
sport
And every country craft, and of us
all
Most courteous to slow age and hasty
youth,
Is dead.

GOATHERD

The boy that brings my griddle
cake
Brought the bare news.

SHEPHERD

He had thrown the crook away
And died in the great war beyond the
sea.

GOATHERD

He had often played his pipes among
my hills,

And when he played it was their
loneliness,
The exultation of their stone, that cried
Under his fingers.

SHEPHERD

I had it from his mother,
And his own flock was browsing at
the door.

GOATHERD

How does she bear her grief? There
is not a shepherd
But grows more gentle when he speaks
her name,
Remembering kindness done, and how
can I,
That found when I had neither goat
nor grazing
New welcome and old wisdom at her fire
Till winter blasts were gone, but speak
of her
Even before his children and his wife.

SHEPHERD

She goes about her house erect and calm
Between the pantry and the linen chest,
Or else at meadow or at grazing overlooks
Her labouring men, as though her darling lived
But for her grandson now; there is no change
But such as I have seen upon her face
Watching our shepherd sports at harvest-time
When her son's turn was over.

GOATHERD

Sing your song,
I too have rhymed my reveries, but youth
Is hot to show whatever it has found,

And till that's done can neither work
nor wait.
Old goatherds and old goats, if in all
else
Youth can excel them in accomplish-
ment,
Are learned in waiting.

SHEPHERD

You cannot but have seen
That he alone had gathered up no gear,
Set carpenters to work on no wide
table,
On no long bench nor lofty milking
shed
As others will, when first they take
possession,
But left the house as in his father's
time
As though he knew himself, as it were,
a cuckoo,
No settled man. And now that he is
gone

There's nothing of him left but half
a score
Of sorrowful, austere, sweet, lofty pipe
tunes.

GOATHERD

You have put the thought in rhyme.

SHEPHERD

I worked all day,
And when 'twas done so little had I
done
That maybe 'I am sorry' in plain
prose
Had sounded better to your mountain
fancy.

[*He sings.*

'Like the speckled bird that steers
Thousands of leagues oversea,
And runs for a while or a while half-
flies
Upon his yellow legs through our
meadows,

He stayed for a while; and we
Had scarcely accustomed our ears
To his speech at the break of day,
Had scarcely accustomed our eyes
To his shape in the lengthening shadows,
Where the sheep are thrown in the pool,
When he vanished from ears and eyes.
I had wished a dear thing on that day
I heard him first, but man is a fool.'

GOATHERD

You sing as always of the natural life,
And I that made like music in my youth
Hearing it now have sighed for that young man
And certain lost companions of my own.

SHEPHERD

They say that on your barren mountain ridge
You have measured out the road that the soul treads
When it has vanished from our natural eyes;
That you have talked with apparitions.

GOATHERD

Indeed
My daily thoughts since the first stupor of youth
Have found the path my goats' feet cannot find.

SHEPHERD

Sing, for it may be that your thoughts have plucked
Some medicable herb to make our grief
Less bitter.

GOATHERD

They have brought me from that ridge
Seed pods and flowers that are not all wild poppy.

[*Sings.*

'He grows younger every second
That were all his birthdays reckoned
Much too solemn seemed;
Because of what he had dreamed,
Or the ambitions that he served,
Much too solemn and reserved.
Jaunting, journeying
To his own dayspring,
He unpacks the loaded pern
Of all 'twas pain or joy to learn,
Of all that he had made.
The outrageous war shall fade;
At some old winding whitethorn root
He'll practise on the shepherd's flute,
Or on the close-cropped grass
Court his shepherd lass,

Or run where lads reform our day-
time
Till that is their long shouting play-
time;
Knowledge he shall unwind
Through victories of the mind,
Till, clambering at the cradle side,
He dreams himself his mother's pride,
All knowledge lost in trance
Of sweeter ignorance.'

SHEPHERD

When I have shut these ewes and this
old ram
Into the fold, we'll to the woods and
there
Cut out our rhymes on strips of new-
torn bark
But put no name and leave them at
her door.
To know the mountain and the
valley grieve

May be a quiet thought to wife and
mother,
And children when they spring up
shoulder high.

LINES WRITTEN IN DEJECTION

WHEN have I last looked on
The round green eyes and the long
wavering bodies
Of the dark leopards of the moon ?
All the wild witches those most noble
ladies,
For all their broom-sticks and their
tears,
Their angry tears, are gone.
The holy centaurs of the hills are
banished ;
And I have nothing but harsh sun ;
Heroic mother moon has vanished,
And now that I have come to fifty
years
I must endure the timid sun.

THE DAWN

I WOULD be ignorant as the dawn
That has looked down
On that old queen measuring a town
With the pin of a brooch,
Or on the withered men that saw
From their pedantic Babylon
The careless planets in their courses,
The stars fade out where the moon
comes,
And took their tablets and did sums;
I would be ignorant as the dawn
That merely stood, rocking the glitter-
ing coach
Above the cloudy shoulders of the
horses;
I would be—for no knowledge is
worth a straw—
Ignorant and wanton as the dawn.

ON WOMAN

May God be praised for woman
That gives up all her mind,
A man may find in no man
A friendship of her kind
That covers all he has brought
As with her flesh and bone,
Nor quarrels with a thought
Because it is not her own.

Though pedantry denies
It's plain the Bible means
That Solomon grew wise
While talking with his queens
Yet never could, although
They say he counted grass,
Count all the praises due

When Sheba was his lass,
When she the iron wrought, or
When from the smithy fire
It shuddered in the water :
Harshness of their desire
That made them stretch and yawn,
Pleasure that comes with sleep,
Shudder that made them one.
What else He give or keep
God grant me—no not here,
For I am not so bold
To hope a thing so dear
Now I am growing old,
But when if the tale's true
The Pestle of the moon
That pounds up all anew
Brings me to birth again—
To find what once I had
And know what once I have known,
Until I am driven mad,
Sleep driven from my bed,
By tenderness and care,
Pity, an aching head,

Gnashing of teeth, despair;
And all because of some one
Perverse creature of chance,
And live like Solomon
That Sheba led a dance.

THE FISHERMAN

Although I can see him still
The freckled man who goes
To a grey place on a hill
In grey Connemara clothes
At dawn to cast his flies,
It's long since I began
To call up to the eyes
This wise and simple man.
All day I'd looked in the face
What I had hoped 'twould be
To write for my own race
And the reality;
The living men that I hate,
The dead man that I loved,
The craven man in his seat,
The insolent unreproved
And no knave brought to book
Who has won a drunken cheer,

The witty man and his joke
Aimed at the commonest ear,
The clever man who cries
The catch-cries of the clown,
The beating down of the wise
And great Art beaten down.

Maybc a twelvemonth since
Suddenly I began,
In scorn of this audience
Imagining a man,
And his sun-freckled face,
And grey Connemara cloth,
Climbing up to a place
Where stone is dark under froth,
And the down turn of his wrist
When the flies drop in the stream;
A man who does not exist,
A man who is but a dream;
And cried, 'Before I am old
I shall have written him one
Poem maybe as cold
And passionate as the dawn.'

THE HAWK

'Call down the hawk from the air;
Let him be hooded or caged
Till the yellow eye has grown mild,
For larder and spit are bare,
The old cook enraged,
The scullion gone wild.'

'I will not be clapped in a hood,
Nor a cage, nor alight upon wrist,
Now I have learnt to be proud
Hovering over the wood
In the broken mist
Or tumbling cloud.'

'What tumbling cloud did you cleave,
Yellow-eyed hawk of the mind,
Last evening? that I, who had sat
Dumbfounded before a knave,
Should give to my friend
A pretence of wit.'

MEMORY

ONE had a lovely face,
And two or three had charm,
But charm and face were in vain
Because the mountain grass
Cannot but keep the form
Where the mountain hare has lain.

HER PRAISE

SHE is foremost of those that I would
hear praised.
I have gone about the house, gone up
and down
As a man does who has published a
new book
Or a young girl dressed out in her new
gown,
And though I have turned the talk by
hook or crook
Until her praise should be the upper-
most theme,
A woman spoke of some new tale she
had read,
A man confusedly in a half dream
As though some other name ran in
his head.

She is foremost of those that I would
hear praised.
I will talk no more of books or the long
war
But walk by the dry thorn until I
have found
Some beggar sheltering from the wind,
and there
Manage the talk until her name come
round.
If there be rags enough he will know
her name
And be well pleased remembering it,
for in the old days,
Though she had young men's praise
and old men's blame,
Among the poor both old and young
gave her praise.

THE PEOPLE

'WHAT have I earned for all that work,' I said,
'For all that I have done at my own charge?
The daily spite of this unmannerly town,
Where who has served the most is most defamed,
The reputation of his lifetime lost
Between the night and morning. I might have lived,
And you know well how great the longing has been,
Where every day my footfall should have lit
In the green shadow of Ferrara wall;

Or climbed among the images of the
past—
The unperturbed and courtly images—
Evening and morning, the steep street
of Urbino
To where the duchess and her people
talked
The stately midnight through until
they stood
In their great window looking at the
dawn ;
I might have had no friend that could
not mix
Courtesy and passion into one like
those
That saw the wicks grow yellow in the
dawn ;
I might have used the one substantial
right
My trade allows : chosen my com-
pany,
And chosen what scenery had pleased
me best.'

Thereon my phoenix answered in reproof,
'The drunkards, pilferers of public funds,
All the dishonest crowd I had driven away,
When my luck changed and they dared meet my face,
Crawled from obscurity, and set upon me
Those I had served and some that I had fed;
Yet never have I, now nor any time,
Complained of the people.'

All I could reply
Was: 'You, that have not lived in thought but deed,
Can have the purity of a natural force,
But I, whose virtues are the definitions
Of the analytic mind, can neither close
The eye of the mind nor keep my tongue from speech.'

And yet, because my heart leaped at
her words,
I was abashed, and now they come
to mind
After nine years, I sink my head
abashed.

HIS PHOENIX

There is a queen in China, or maybe it's in Spain,
And birthdays and holidays such praises can be heard
Of her unblemished lineaments, a whiteness with no stain,
That she might be that sprightly girl who was trodden by a bird;
And there's a score of duchesses, surpassing womankind,
Or who have found a painter to make them so for pay
And smooth out stain and blemish with the elegance of his mind:
I knew a phoenix in my youth so let them have their day.

The young men every night applaud
their Gaby's laughing eye,
And Ruth St. Denis had more charm
although she had poor luck,
From nineteen hundred nine or ten,
Pavlova's had the cry,
And there's a player in the States who
gathers up her cloak
And flings herself out of the room when
Juliet would be bride
With all a woman's passion, a child's
imperious way,
And there are—but no matter if there
are scores beside :
I knew a phoenix in my youth so let
them have their day.

There's Margaret and Marjorie and
Dorothy and Nan,
A Daphne and a Mary who live in
privacy ;
One's had her fill of lovers, another's
had but one,

Another boasts, 'I pick and choose
and have but two or three.'
If head and limb have beauty and the
instep's high and light
They can spread out what sail they
please for all I have to say,
Be but the breakers of men's hearts or
engines of delight :
I knew a phoenix in my youth so let
them have their day.

There'll be that crowd to make men
wild through all the centuries,
And maybe there'll be some young
belle walk out to make men wild
Who is my beauty's equal, though that
my heart denies,
But not the exact likeness, the sim-
plicity of a child,
And that proud look as though she
had gazed into the burning sun,
And all the shapely body no tittle gone
astray,

I mourn for that most lonely thing;
    and yet God's will be done,
I knew a phoenix in my youth so let
    them have their day.

A THOUGHT FROM PROPERTIUS

SHE might, so noble from head
To great shapely knees
The long flowing line,
Have walked to the altar
Through the holy images
At Pallas Athene's side,
Or been fit spoil for a centaur
Drunk with the unmixed wine.

BROKEN DREAMS

THERE is grey in your hair.
Young men no longer suddenly catch
their breath
When you are passing;
But maybe some old gaffer mutters a
blessing
Because it was your prayer
Recovered him upon the bed of death.
For your sole sake—that all heart's
ache have known,
And given to others all heart's ache,
From meagre girlhood's putting on
Burdensome beauty—for your sole
sake
Heaven has put away the stroke of her
doom,

So great her portion in that peace you
make
By merely walking in a room.

Your beauty can but leave among us
Vague memories, nothing but memories.
A young man when the old men are
done talking
Will say to an old man, 'Tell me of
that lady
The poet stubborn with his passion
sang us
When age might well have chilled his
blood.'

Vague memories, nothing but memories,
But in the grave all, all, shall be
renewed.
The certainty that I shall see that
lady
Leaning or standing or walking

In the first loveliness of womanhood,
And with the fervour of my youthful eyes,
Has set me muttering like a fool.

You are more beautiful than any one
And yet your body had a flaw:
Your small hands were not beautiful,
And I am afraid that you will run
And paddle to the wrist
In that mysterious, always brimming lake
Where those that have obeyed the holy law
Paddle and are perfect; leave unchanged
The hands that I have kissed
For old sakes' sake.

The last stroke of midnight dies.
All day in the one chair

From dream to dream and rhyme to
rhyme I have ranged
In rambling talk with an image of air :
Vague memories, nothing but memories.

A DEEP-SWORN VOW

OTHERS because you did not keep
That deep-sworn vow have been friends
of mine;
Yet always when I look death in the
face,
When I clamber to the heights of
sleep,
Or when I grow excited with wine,
Suddenly I meet your face.

PRESENCES

THIS night has been so strange that it
seemed
As if the hair stood up on my head.
From going-down of the sun I have
dreamed
That women laughing, or timid or
wild,
In rustle of lace or silken stuff,
Climbed up my creaking stair. They
had read
All I had rhymed of that monstrous
thing
Returned and yet unrequited love.
They stood in the door and stood
between
My great wood lecturn and the fire

Till I could hear their hearts beating:
One is a harlot, and one a child
That never looked upon man with
desire,
And one it may be a queen.

THE BALLOON OF THE MIND

HANDS do what you're bid;
Bring the balloon of the mind
That bellies and drags in the wind
Into its narrow shed.

TO A SQUIRREL AT KYLE-NA-GNO

COME play with me;
Why should you run
Through the shaking tree
As though I'd a gun
To strike you dead?
When all I would do
Is to scratch your head
And let you go.

ON BEING ASKED FOR A WAR POEM

I THINK it better that in times like these
A poet keep his mouth shut, for in truth
We have no gift to set a statesman right;
He has had enough of meddling who can please
A young girl in the indolence of her youth,
Or an old man upon a winter's night.

IN MEMORY OF ALFRED POLLEXFEN

FIVE-AND-TWENTY years have gone
Since old William Pollexfen
Laid his strong bones down in death
By his wife Elizabeth
In the grey stone tomb he made.
And after twenty years they laid
In that tomb by him and her,
His son George, the astrologer;
And Masons drove from miles away
To scatter the Acacia spray
Upon a melancholy man
Who had ended where his breath
began.
Many a son and daughter lies
Far from the customary skies,

The Mall and Eades's grammar school,
In London or in Liverpool;
But where is laid the sailor John?
That so many lands had known:
Quiet lands or unquiet seas
Where the Indians trade or Japanese.
He never found his rest ashore
Moping for one voyage more.
Where have they laid the sailor John?

And yesterday the youngest son,
A humorous, unambitious man,
Was buried near the astrologer;
And are we now in the tenth year?
Since he, who had been contented
long,
A nobody in a great throng,
Decided he would journey home,
Now that his fiftieth year had come,
And 'Mr. Alfred' be again
Upon the lips of common men
Who carried in their memory
His childhood and his family.

At all these death-beds women heard
A visionary white sea-bird
Lamenting that a man should die;
And with that cry I have raised my
cry.

UPON A DYING LADY

I

HER COURTESY

With the old kindness, the old distinguished grace
She lies, her lovely piteous head amid dull red hair
Propped upon pillows, rouge on the pallor of her face.
She would not have us sad because she is lying there,
And when she meets our gaze her eyes are laughter-lit,
Her speech a wicked tale that we may vie with her

Matching our broken-hearted wit
against her wit,
Thinking of saints and of Petronius
Arbiter.

II

CERTAIN ARTISTS BRING HER
DOLLS AND DRAWINGS

Bring where our Beauty lies
A new modelled doll, or drawing,
With a friend's or an enemy's
Features, or maybe showing
Her features when a tress
Of dull red hair was flowing
Over some silken dress
Cut in the Turkish fashion,
Or it may be like a boy's.
We have given the world our passion,
We have naught for death but toys.

III

SHE TURNS THE DOLLS' FACES TO THE WALL

Because to-day is some religious
festival
They had a priest say Mass, and even
the Japanese,
Heel up and weight on toe, must face
the wall
—Pedant in passion, learned in old
courtesies,
Vehement and witty she had seemed—;
the Venetian lady
Who had seemed to glide to some in-
trigue in her red shoes,
Her domino, her panniered skirt copied
from Longhi ;
The meditative critic ; all are on their
toes,
Even our Beauty with her Turkish
trousers on.

Because the priest must have like every dog his day
Or keep us all awake with baying at the moon,
We and our dolls being but the world were best away.

IV

THE END OF DAY

She is playing like a child
And penance is the play,
Fantastical and wild
Because the end of day
Shows her that some one soon
Will come from the house, and say—
Though play is but half-done—
'Come in and leave the play.'—

V

HER RACE

She has not grown uncivil
As narrow natures would

And called the pleasures evil
Happier days thought good ;
She knows herself a woman
No red and white of a face,
Or rank, raised from a common
Unreckonable race ;
And how should her heart fail her
Or sickness break her will
With her dead brother's valour
For an example still.

VI

HER COURAGE

When her soul flies to the predestined
dancing-place
(I have no speech but symbol, the
pagan speech I made
Amid the dreams of youth) let her
come face to face,
While wondering still to be a shade,
with Grania's shade

All but the perils of the woodland flight forgot
That made her Dermuid dear, and some old cardinal
Pacing with half-closed eyelids in a sunny spot
Who had murmured of Giorgione at his latest breath—
Aye and Achilles, Timor, Babar, Barhaim all
Who have lived in joy and laughed into the face of Death.

VII

HER FRIENDS BRING HER A CHRISTMAS TREE

Pardon great enemy,
Without an angry thought
We've carried in our tree,
And here and there have bought
Till all the boughs are gay,
And she may look from the bed

On pretty things that may
Please a fantastic head.
Give her a little grace,
What if a laughing eye
Have looked into your face—
It is about to die.

EGO DOMINUS TUUS

Hic

On the grey sand beside the shallow
stream
Under your old wind-beaten tower,
where still
A lamp burns on beside the open
book
That Michael Robartes left, you walk
in the moon
And though you have passed the best
of life still trace
Enthralled by the unconquerable de-
lusion
Magical shapes.

ILLE

By the help of an image
I call to my own opposite, summon all
That I have handled least, least looked
upon.

HIC

And I would find myself and not an
image.

ILLE

That is our modern hope and by its
light
We have lit upon the gentle, sensitive
mind
And lost the old nonchalance of the
hand ;
Whether we have chosen chisel, pen
or brush
We are but critics, or but half create
Timid, entangled, empty and abashed
Lacking the countenance of our friends.

HIC

And yet
The chief imagination of Christendom
Dante Alighieri so utterly found himself
That he has made that hollow face of his
More plain to the mind's eye than any face
But that of Christ.

ILLE

And did he find himself
Or was the hunger that had made it hollow
A hunger for the apple on the bough
Most out of reach ? and is that spectral image
The man that Lapo and that Guido knew ?
I think he fashioned from his opposite
An image that might have been a stony face,

Staring upon a bedouin's horse-hair roof
From doored and windowed cliff, or half upturned
Among the coarse grass and the camel dung.
He set his chisel to the hardest stone.
Being mocked by Guido for his lecherous life
Derided and deriding, driven out
To climb that stair and eat that bitter bread,
He found the unpersuadable justice, he found
The most exalted lady loved by a man.

HIC

Yet surely there are men who have made their art
Out of no tragic war, lovers of life,
Impulsive men that look for happiness
And sing when they have found it.

ILLE

No not sing,
For those that love the world serve it in action,
Grow rich, popular and full of influence,
And should they paint or write still it is action :
The struggle of the fly in marmalade.
The rhetorician would deceive his neighbours,
The sentimentalist himself ; while art
Is but a vision of reality.
What portion in the world can the artist have
Who has awakened from the common dream
But dissipation and despair ?

HIC

And yet
No one denies to Keats love of the world ;
Remember his deliberate happiness.

Ille

His art is happy but who knows his
mind?
I see a schoolboy when I think of him
With face and nose pressed to a sweet-
shop window,
For certainly he sank into his grave
His senses and his heart unsatisfied,
And made—being poor, ailing and
ignorant,
Shut out from all the luxury of the
world,
The coarse-bred son of a livery stable-
keeper—
Luxuriant song.

Hic

Why should you leave the lamp
Burning alone beside an open book,
And trace these characters upon the
sands?
A style is found by sedentary toil
And by the imitation of great masters.

ILLE

Because I seek an image not a book.
Those men that in their writings are
most wise
Own nothing but their blind, stupefied
hearts.
I call to the mysterious one who yet
Shall walk the wet sands by the edge
of the stream
And look most like me, being indeed
my double,
And prove of all imaginable things
The most unlike, being my anti-self,
And standing by these characters
disclose
All that I seek; and whisper it as
though
He were afraid the birds, who cry aloud
Their momentary cries before it is
dawn,
Would carry it away to blasphemous
men.

A PRAYER ON GOING INTO MY HOUSE

God grant a blessing on this tower and cottage
And on my heirs, if all remain unspoiled,
No table, or chair or stool not simple enough
For shepherd lads in Galilee; and grant
That I myself for portions of the year
May handle nothing and set eyes on nothing
But what the great and passionate have used
Throughout so many varying centuries.

We take it for the norm; yet should
I dream
Sinbad the sailor's brought a painted
chest,
Or image, from beyond the Loadstone
Mountain,
That dream is a norm; and should
some limb of the devil
Destroy the view by cutting down an
ash
That shades the road, or setting up a
cottage
Planned in a government office,
shorten his life,
Manacle his soul upon the Red Sea
bottom.

THE PHASES OF THE MOON

An old man cocked his ear upon a bridge;
He and his friend, their faces to the South,
Had trod the uneven road. Their boots were soiled,
Their Connemara cloth worn out of shape;
They had kept a steady pace as though their beds,
Despite a dwindling and late risen moon,
Were distant. An old man cocked his ear.

AHERNE

WHAT made that sound?

ROBARTES

A rat or water-hen
Splashed, or an otter slid into the stream.
We are on the bridge; that shadow is the tower,
And the light proves that he is reading still.
He has found, after the manner of his kind,
Mere images; chosen this place to live in
Because, it may be, of the candle light
From the far tower where Milton's platonist
Sat late, or Shelley's visionary prince:
The lonely light that Samuel Palmer engraved,
An image of mysterious wisdom won by toil;
And now he seeks in book or manuscript
What he shall never find.

Aherne

Why should not you
Who know it all ring at his door, and speak
Just truth enough to show that his whole life
Will scarcely find for him a broken crust
Of all those truths that are your daily bread;
And when you have spoken take the roads again?

Robartes

He wrote of me in that extravagant style
He had learnt from Pater, and to round his tale
Said I was dead; and dead I chose to be.

AHERNE

Sing me the changes of the moon once
more;
True song, though speech: 'mine
author sung it me.'

ROBARTES

Twenty-and-eight the phases of the
moon,
The full and the moon's dark and all
the crescents,
Twenty-and-eight, and yet but six-
and-twenty
The cradles that a man must needs be
rocked in:
For there's no human life at the full
or the dark.
From the first crescent to the half, the
dream
But summons to adventure and the
man

Is always happy like a bird or a beast;
But while the moon is rounding towards the full
He follows whatever whim's most difficult
Among whims not impossible, and though scarred,
As with the cat-o'-nine-tails of the mind,
His body moulded from within his body
Grows comelier. Eleven pass, and then
Athenae takes Achilles by the hair,
Hector is in the dust, Nietzsche is born,
Because the heroes' crescent is the twelfth.
And yet, twice born, twice buried, grow he must,
Before the full moon, helpless as a worm.
The thirteenth moon but sets the soul at war

In its own being, and when that war's begun
There is no muscle in the arm; and after
Under the frenzy of the fourteenth moon
The soul begins to tremble into stillness,
To die into the labyrinth of itself!

AHERNE

Sing out the song; sing to the end, and sing
The strange reward of all that discipline.

ROBARTES

All thought becomes an image and the soul
Becomes a body: that body and that soul
Too perfect at the full to lie in a cradle,

Too lonely for the traffic of the world:
Body and soul cast out and cast away
Beyond the visible world.

AHERNE

All dreams of the soul
End in a beautiful man's or woman's body.

RÓBARTES

Have you not always known it?

AHERNE

The song will have it
That those that we have loved got their long fingers
From death, and wounds, or on Sinai's top,
Or from some bloody whip in their own hands.
They ran from cradle to cradle till at last

Their beauty dropped out of the loneliness
Of body and soul.

ROBARTES

The lovers' heart knows that.

AHERNE

It must be that the terror in their eyes
Is memory or foreknowledge of the hour
When all is fed with light and heaven is bare.

ROBARTES

When the moon's full those creatures of the full
Are met on the waste hills by country men
Who shudder and hurry by: body and soul
Estranged amid the strangeness of themselves,

Caught up in contemplation, the mind's eye
Fixed upon images that once were thought,
For separate, perfect, and immovable
Images can break the solitude
Of lovely, satisfied, indifferent eyes.

And thereupon with aged, high-pitched voice
Aherne laughed, thinking of the man within,
His sleepless candle and laborious pen.

ROBARTES

And after that the crumbling of the moon.
The soul remembering its loneliness
Shudders in many cradles; all is changed,
It would be the world's servant, and as it serves,

Choosing whatever task's most difficult
Among tasks not impossible, it takes
Upon the body and upon the soul
The coarseness of the drudge.

Aherne

Before the full
It sought itself and afterwards the world.

Robartes

Because you are forgotten, half out of life,
And never wrote a book your thought is clear.
Reformer, merchant, statesman, learned man,
Dutiful husband, honest wife by turn,
Cradle upon cradle, and all in flight and all
Deformed because there is no deformity
But saves us from a dream.

AHERNE

And what of those
That the last servile crescent has set
free ?

ROBARTES

Because all dark, like those that are
all light,
They are cast beyond the verge, and
in a cloud,
Crying to one another like the bats ;
And having no desire they cannot tell
What's good or bad, or what it is to
triumph
At the perfection of one's own obedi-
ence ;
And yet they speak what's blown into
the mind ;
Deformed beyond deformity, un-
formed,
Insipid as the dough before it is baked,
They change their bodies at a word.

AHERNE

And then?

ROBARTES

When all the dough has been so kneaded up
That it can take what form cook Nature fancy
The first thin crescent is wheeled round once more.

AHERNE

But the escape; the song's not finished yet.

ROBARTES

Hunchback and saint and fool are the last crescents.
The burning bow that once could shoot an arrow
Out of the up and down, the wagon wheel

Of beauty's cruelty and wisdom's chatter,
Out of that raving tide is drawn betwixt
Deformity of body and of mind.

AHERNE

Were not our beds far off I'd ring the bell,
Stand under the rough roof-timbers of the hall
Beside the castle door, where all is stark
Austerity, a place set out for wisdom
That he will never find; I'd play a part;
He would never know me after all these years
But take me for some drunken country man;
I'd stand and mutter there until he caught

'Hunchback and saint and fool,' and
that they came
Under the three last crescents of the
moon,
And then I'd stagger out. He'd crack
his wits
Day after day, yet never find the
meaning.

And then he laughed to think that what
seemed hard
Should be so simple—a bat rose from
the hazels
And circled round him with its squeaky
cry,
The light in the tower window was put
out.

THE CAT AND THE MOON

THE cat went here and there
And the moon spun round like a top,
And the nearest kin of the moon
The creeping cat looked up.
Black Minnaloushe stared at the moon,
For wander and wail as he would
The pure cold light in the sky
Troubled his animal blood.
Minnaloushe runs in the grass
Lifting his delicate feet.
Do you dance, Minnaloushe, do you
dance ?
When two close kindred meet
What better than call a dance,
Maybe the moon may learn,
Tired of that courtly fashion,

A new dance turn.
Minnaloushe creeps through the grass
From moonlit place to place,
The sacred moon overhead
Has taken a new phase.
Does Minnaloushe know that his pupils
Will pass from change to change,
And that from round to crescent,
From crescent to round they range?
Minnaloushe creeps through the grass
Alone, important and wise,
And lifts to the changing moon
His changing eyes.

THE SAINT AND THE HUNCHBACK

HUNCHBACK

STAND up and lift your hand and
bless
A man that finds great bitterness
In thinking of his lost renown.
A Roman Caesar is held down
Under this hump.

SAINT

God tries each man
According to a different plan.
I shall not cease to bless because
I lay about me with the taws
That night and morning I may thrash

Greek Alexander from my flesh,
Augustus Caesar, and after these
That great rogue Alcibiades.

HUNCHBACK

To all that in your flesh have stood
And blessed, I give my gratitude,
Honoured by all in their degrees,
But most to Alcibiades.

TWO SONGS OF A FOOL

I

A SPECKLED cat and a tame hare
Eat at my hearthstone
And sleep there ;
And both look up to me alone
For learning and defence
As I look up to Providence.

I start out of my sleep to think
Some day I may forget
Their food and drink ;
Or, the house door left unshut,
The hare may run till it's found
The horn's sweet note and the tooth
of the hound.

I bear a burden that might well try
Men that do all by rule,

And what can I
That am a wandering witted fool
But pray to God that He ease
My great responsibilities.

II

I slept on my three-legged stool by
the fire,
The speckled cat slept on my knee ;
We never thought to enquire
Where the brown hare might be,
And whether the door were shut.
Who knows how she drank the wind
Stretched up on two legs from the mat,
Before she had settled her mind
To drum with her heel and to leap :
Had I but awakened from sleep
And called her name she had heard,
It may be, and had not stirred,
That now, it may be, has found
The horn's sweet note and the tooth
of the hound.

ANOTHER SONG OF A FOOL

This great purple butterfly,
In the prison of my hands,
Has a learning in his eye
Not a poor fool understands.

Once he lived a schoolmaster
With a stark, denying look,
A string of scholars went in fear
Of his great birch and his great book.

Like the clangour of a bell,
Sweet and harsh, harsh and sweet,
That is how he learnt so well
To take the roses for his meat.

THE DOUBLE VISION OF MICHAEL ROBARTES

I

On the grey rock of Cashel the mind's
    eye
Has called up the cold spirits that are
    born
When the old moon is vanished from
    the sky
And the new still hides her horn.

Under blank eyes and fingers never
    still
The particular is pounded till it is
    man,
When had I my own will?
Oh, not since life began.

Constrained, arraigned, baffled, bent
and unbent
By these wire-jointed jaws and limbs
of wood,
Themselves obedient,
Knowing not evil and good;

Obedient to some hidden magical
breath.
They do not even feel, so abstract are
they,
So dead beyond our death,
Triumph that we obey.

II

On the grey rock of Cashel I suddenly
saw
A Sphinx with woman breast and lion
paw,
A Buddha, hand at rest,
Hand lifted up that blest;
And right between these two a girl
at play

That it maybe had danced her life
  away,
For now being dead it seemed
That she of dancing dreamed.

Although I saw it all in the mind's eye
There can be nothing solider till I die;
I saw by the moon's light
Now at its fifteenth night.

One lashed her tail; her eyes lit by
  the moon
Gazed upon all things known, all
  things unknown,
In triumph of intellect
With motionless head erect.

That other's moonlit eyeballs never
  moved,
Being fixed on all things loved, all
  things unloved,
Yet little peace he had
For those that love are sad.

Oh, little did they care who danced between,
And little she by whom her dance was seen
So that she danced. No thought,
Body perfection brought,

For what but eye and ear silence the mind
With the minute particulars of mankind ?
Mind moved yet seemed to stop
As 'twere a spinning-top.

In contemplation had those three so wrought
Upon a moment, and so stretched it out
That they, time overthrown,
Were dead yet flesh and bone.

III

I knew that I had seen, had seen at
last
That girl my unremembering nights
hold fast
Or else my dreams that fly,
If I should rub an eye,

And yet in flying fling into my
meat
A crazy juice that makes the pulses
beat
As though I had been undone
By Homer's Paragon

Who never gave the burning town a
thought;
To such a pitch of folly I am
brought,
Being caught between the pull
Of the dark moon and the full,

The commonness of thought and
    images
That have the frenzy of our western
    seas.
Thereon I made my moan,
And after kissed a stone,

And after that arranged it in a song
Seeing that I, ignorant for so long,
Had been rewarded thus
In Cormac's ruined house.

NOTE

"*Unpack the loaded pern,*" p. 36.

When I was a child at Sligo I could see above my grandfather's trees a little column of smoke from "the pern mill," and was told that "pern" was another name for the spool, as I was accustomed to call it, on which thread was wound. One could not see the chimney for the trees, and the smoke looked as if it came from the mountain, and one day a foreign sea-captain asked me if that was a burning mountain.

W. B. Y.

Printed by R. & R. CLARK, LIMITED *Edinburgh*.

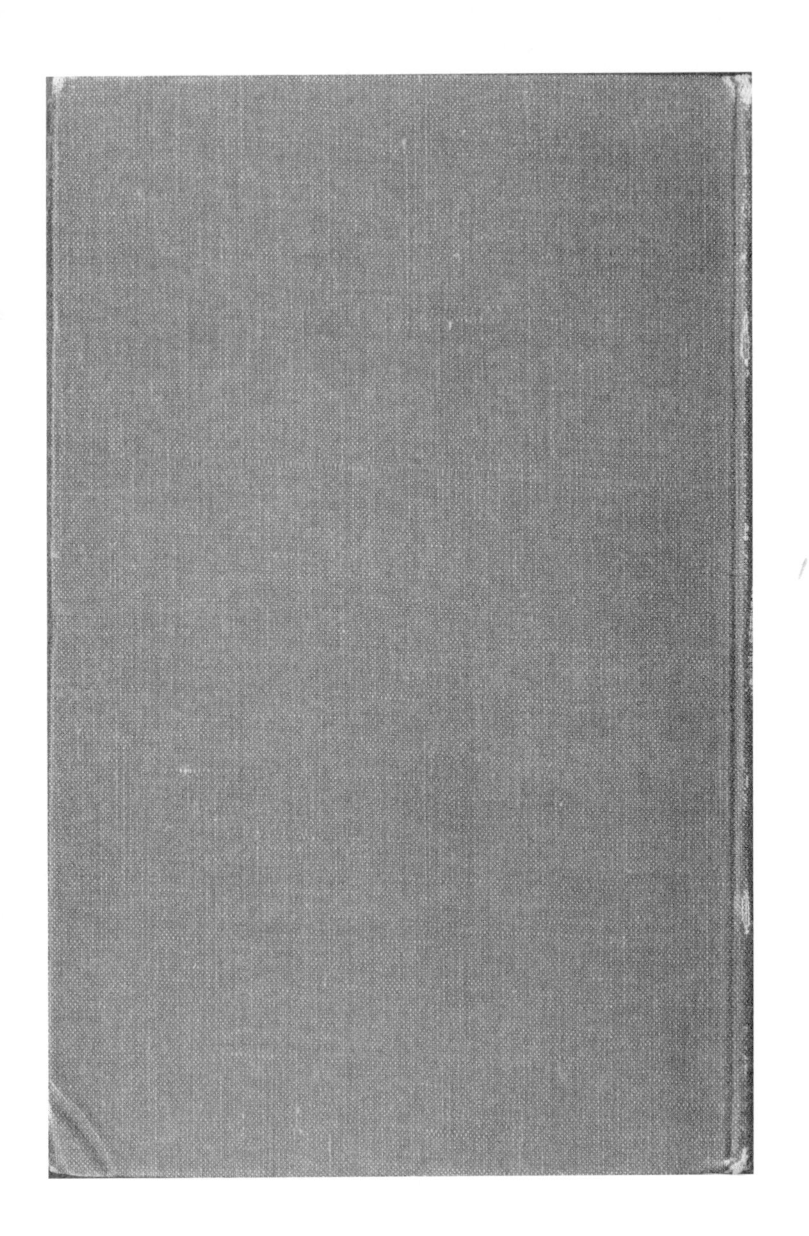

NOTES

PREFACE

The Wild Swans at Coole: Other Verses and a Play in Verse was first published by the Cuala Press (Churchtown, Ireland, 1917). For the revised 1919 edition, published by Macmillan and used for this facsimile edition, Yeats cut the Cuchulain play *At the Hawk's Well* (later included in *Four Plays for Dancers* and elsewhere). He also added to the original poems seventeen others, including those related to Robert Gregory, Iseult Gonne, and his wife, Georgie, near the beginning of the book to his evolving system for *A Vision* near the end.

Robartes and Aherne are fictional characters invented by Yeats as early as the 1890s. In the present volume, they appear most prominently in "Ego Dominus Tuus," "The Phases of the Moon," and "The Double Vision of Michael Robartes." The "disturbance" (actually closer to a riot) took place at the first production of John Synge's play *The Playboy of the Western World* at the Abbey Theatre in 1907. Now regarded as a masterpiece, the play offended narrow nationalist sympathies of the time. Ballylee, near Coole in County Galway, was the old Norman tower that Yeats bought and restored; he lived there for ten summers with his family.

THE WILD SWANS AT COOLE

First published in *The Little Review*, June 1917, where the current last stanza came third, thus changing the thrust and meaning of the poem to make it more defeatist.

Coole Park, in County Galway near the town of Gort, was the estate of Yeats's patron, friend, and collaborator Lady Gregory. He first visited there briefly in 1896 and stayed for more extended periods from the summer of 1897 onward. "I found at last what I had been seeking always, a life of order and of labour," he later wrote. See, among other works, the two poems "Coole Park, 1929" and "Coole and Ballylee, 1931" from *The Winding Stair and Other Poems* (1933).

IN MEMORY OF MAJOR ROBERT GREGORY

First published in *The English Review*, August 1918; *The Little Review*, September 1918.

Yeats's note after the title in *The Little Review* read: "Major Robert Gregory, R.F.C., M.C., Legion of Honour, was killed in action on the Italian Front, January 23, 1918." Gregory (1881–1918) was Lady Gregory's only child, shot down by friendly fire from an Italian airman during World War I. See in the present volume "An Irish Airman Foresees His Death" and "Shepherd and Goatherd," as well as the poem "Reprisals," not published until after Lady Gregory's own death.

1–3: "Our house" was the tower at Ballylee, which the Yeatses were having renovated while they stayed nearby at Ballinamantane House, owned by Lady Gregory. The tower's floors are connected by a narrow winding stair.

17: Lionel Johnson (1867–1902) was an Irish poet and member, with Yeats and others, of the Rhymers' Club during the 1890s; he impressed Yeats with his learning as well as with poems like "The Dark Angel."

25: John Synge (1871–1909), Irish playwright and friend to Yeats, set much of his work in the West of Ireland, including his famous *The Playboy of the Western World.*

33: George Pollexfen (1839–1910) was a maternal uncle of Yeats who lived in Sligo, just north of County Mayo. A steeplechase racer in his youth, he later delved into astrology. Sir Philip Sidney (1554–86) was an English Renaissance writer, diplomat, and soldier, often taken as an archetype of the Renaissance gentleman. Like Robert Gregory, he died in battle in his thirties.

57f: Stanza 8 was added at the request of Gregory's widow. Galway is a county in western Ireland. Castle Taylor was the childhood home of Lady Gregory (née Persse). Esserkelly and Mooneen are near Ardrahan.

66: County Clare is directly south of County Galway.

AN IRISH AIRMAN FORESEES HIS DEATH

First published in *The Wild Swans at Coole* (London and New York), 1919. The "Irish Airman" is Major Robert Gregory, Lady Gregory's only son.

5–6: Kiltartan Cross is a crossroads near Coole in County Galway. Lady Gregory did a series of translations of Irish folktales set near there.

MEN IMPROVE WITH THE YEARS

First published in *The Little Review*, June 1917. The poem is one of several resulting from Yeats's infatuation with Maud Gonne's daughter, Iseult.

2: In Greek legend, tritons or mermen were sea gods, often represented as bearded men with the hindquarters of fish.

THE COLLAR-BONE OF A HARE

First published in *The Little Review,* June 1917.

UNDER THE ROUND TOWER

First published in *The Little Review*, October 1918.

Title: Thin round towers were built in Ireland from about the ninth century to defend against Scandinavian raiders.

4–9: Many Byrnes and O'Byrnes are associated with the landscape around Glendalough in County Wicklow. One of them, William Byrne of Ballymanus, was a Wicklow hero hanged for his role in the 1798 Rising. Glendalough ("glen of the two lakes") is a famous monastic site in the Wicklow mountains associated with St. Kevin (d. 618).

SOLOMON TO SHEBA

First published in *The Little Review*, October 1918. In the Bible, King Solomon (ca. 972–ca. 932 BCE) ruled the Hebrews and was an archetype of the wise ruler. I Kings 10:1–13 describes the visit to King Solomon of the Queen of Sheba, an area in southern Arabia. In the poem the two also represent Yeats and his wife exploring love and esoteric knowledge.

THE LIVING BEAUTY

First published in *The Little Review*, October 1918. Like the following three poems, it grows out of Yeats's experience with Iseult Gonne and her mother, Maud.

A SONG

First published in *The Little Review*, October 1918.

TO A YOUNG BEAUTY

First published in *Nine Poems* (London, 1918).

11–12: The biblical prophet Ezekiel lived during the sixth century BCE. For his cherubim, see especially Ezekiel 10:1–22. Beaujolet was later changed to Beauvarlet; Jacques Firmin Beauvarlet (1731–97) was an eighteenth-century painter and engraver who often included cherubim in his works.

18: Yeats admired the minor Romantic poet Walter Savage Landor (1775–1864) and assigned him to the same phase as himself in *A Vision*. He also admired the Renaissance poet and clergyman John Donne (1572–1631), especially for his ability to combine mind and body.

TO A YOUNG GIRL

First published in *The Little Review*, October 1918. "To a Young Girl" concludes (for now) the series of poems based on Iseult and Maud Gonne. The young girl is based on Iseult and her mother on Maud.

THE SCHOLARS

First published in *Catholic Anthology 1914–1915* (London, 1915). Yeats distrusted formal education, holding that it encouraged conformity and discouraged what he called "Unity of Being." The poet W. H. Auden later rebuked Yeats for scorning those who "edit and annote the lines," saying "thank God they do."

12: Gaius Valerius Catullus (84–54 BCE) was a Roman love poet.

TOM O'ROUGHLEY

First published in *The Little Review*, October 1918. Tom O'Roughley is another of Yeats's inspired folk figures, akin to Crazy Jane and others. Roughley is a village and point of land on the coast near Sligo.

7–8: In a later note to "Meditations in Time of Civil War," Yeats wrote, "I have a ring with a hawk and butterfly upon it, to symbolize the straight road of logic, and so of mechanism, and the crooked road of intuition: 'For wisdom is a butterfly and not a gloomy bird of prey.' "

13: "Trumpeter Michael" is the archangel Michael blowing his horn at the Last Judgment.

THE SAD SHEPHERD

First published in *The Wild Swans at Coole* (London and New York, 1919). This is the third elegy for Robert Gregory in the volume. At different times Yeats announced that the poem was modeled on the English Renaissance poet Edmund Spenser and on the Classical Latin poet Virgil.

23: "The great war beyond the sea": World War I.

26: "His mother": Lady Gregory.

62: "The Speckled Bird" was the title of an early autobiographical novel by Yeats, published posthumously.

LINES WRITTEN IN DEJECTION

First published in *The Wild Swans at Coole* (Churchtown, Ireland: Cuala Press, 1917).

7: In classical mythology, a centaur has the head and torso of a man and the body and legs of a horse. Yeats wrote in his *Autobiographies* that "All art should be a centaur finding in the popular lore its back and strong legs."

THE DAWN

First published in *Poetry* (Chicago), February 1916.

3–4: The horse goddess Macha in Celtic mythology was the mother of twins. Emain Macha was the capital of the northern kingdom of Ulster. The story of Macha's measuring the town boundary with the pin of a brooch comes from Standish James O'Grady's *History of Ireland: Critical and Philosophical* (1881) vol. 1, and is probably apocryphal. Yeats associated astrology with ancient Babylon, in Mesopotamia.

ON WOMAN

First published in *Poetry* (Chicago), February 1916.

10f: For Solomon and Sheba, see "Solomon to Sheba"

above. Note the double entendre in the following lines.

30: "The Pestle of the moon" refers to the twenty-eight stages in Yeats's esoteric system. A mortar is a bowl, and a pestle the small club-shaped object used to grind things up in the mortar.

THE FISHERMAN

First published in *Poetry* (Chicago), February 1916.

4: "grey Connemara clothes": Connemara is a largely wild region in the West of Ireland. In the "Stirring of the Bones" section of his *Autobiographies*, Yeats recorded his disappointment when his tailor informed him that "It takes such a long time getting Connemara cloth, as it has to come all the way from Scotland."

24: "Great art beaten down" likely refers to the controversy over building an art gallery in Dublin to house Lady Gregory's nephew Hugh Lane's collection of art.

THE HAWK

First published in *Poetry* (Chicago), February 1916. In the "Four Years" section of his *Autobiographies*, Yeats advocated what he called "Unity of Being" and contrasted it with "abstraction." He then went on to quote the first stanza of "The Hawk."

MEMORY

First published in *Poetry* (Chicago), February 1916. Another poem about the women in Yeats's life, presumably Olivia Shakespear toward the beginning and Maud Gonne in the last two lines.

HER PRAISE

First published in *Poetry* (Chicago), February 1916. This poem and the next six grow out of Yeats's reflections on his long relationship with Maud Gonne, who turned fifty-three in December of 1919.

11: The "long war" is World War I.

THE PEOPLE

First published in *Poetry* (Chicago), February 1916.

3: "This unmannerly town": Dublin. In contrast, Ferrara (**9**) and Urbino (**12**) are Italian towns that were praised in Baldassare Castiglione's *The Book of the Courtier* (1528) as centers of the arts and of enlightened rule, especially under Ercole d'Este in Ferrara and Guidobaldo da Montefeltro in Urbino. The duchess was Elisabetta Gonzaga (1471–1526), Duchess of Urbino.

6: "Between the night and the morning" is quoted by Ezra Pound in "Villanelle: The Psychological Hour" and first appeared in Yeats's play *The Green Helmet*.

22: "My phoenix" is Maud Gonne (see next poem).

HIS PHOENIX

First published in *Poetry* (Chicago), February 1916.

Title: A phoenix is a legendary bird that periodically perishes in fire and is reborn.

4: The reference is to Leda in Greek myth, whom Zeus visited in the guise of a swan.

9: Gaby Deslys (1881–1920) was a celebrated French singer and music hall artist with a famous set of pearls.

10: Ruth St. Denis (1879–1968) was an American

dancer associated with both Asian and modern dance.

11: Anna Matveyevna Pavlova (1881–1931) was an acclaimed Russian prima ballerina.

12–13: Probably Julia Marlowe (1866–1950), an actress known especially for her roles in Shakespeare's plays, such as *Romeo and Juliet.*

17: A list of Ezra Pound's girlfriends; he married Dorothy Shakespear, daughter of Yeats's former lover Olivia.

A THOUGHT FROM PROPERTIUS

First published in *The Wild Swans at Coole* (Churchtown, Ireland: Cuala Press, 1917). Sextus Propertius (ca. 50–16 BCE) was a Roman love poet. Yeats's poem is loosely based on the second poem of Book Two of his predecessor's work.

6: Pallas Athene was the ancient Greek goddess of wisdom and was associated with virginity, among other things. Yeats linked her to Maud Gonne in the later poem "Beautiful, Lofty Things" and elsewhere.

BROKEN DREAMS

First published in *The Little Review,* June 1917. Another poem to Maud Gonne.

A DEEP-SWORN VOW

First published in *The Little Review*, June 1917.

2: The "vow" was presumably the one made by Gonne never to marry but to have a special and spiritual friendship with Yeats.

PRESENCES

First published in *The Little Review*, June 1917.

THE BALLOON OF THE MIND

First published in *The New Statesman*, September 29, 1917. Compare a passage that Yeats wrote about his school days in the "Reveries" section of his *Autobiographies*: "My thoughts were a great excitement, but when I tried to do anything with them, it was like trying to pack a balloon into a shed in a high wind."

TO A SQUIRREL AT KYLE-NA-GNO

First published in *The New Statesman*, September 29, 1917. Kyle-na-Gno (later revised to Kyle-na-No) is one of the Seven Woods on Lady Gregory's estate at Coole.

ON BEING ASKED FOR A WAR POEM

First published in *The Book of the Homeless*, ed. Edith Wharton (New York and London, 1916). Written during World War I, the original title appeared as "A Reason for Keeping Silent" in the Wharton collection of poems about the war. The second line there began with the colloquial "We poets keep our mouths shut . . ."

IN MEMORY OF ALFRED POLLEXFEN

First published in *The Little Review*, June 1917. The Sligo merchant family of the Pollexfens were Yeats's ancestors on his mother's side. His father, John Butler Yeats, had married Susan Pollexfen in 1863, and WBY was born two years later.

2–4: The fierce William Pollexfen and his gentler wife, Elizabeth, were Yeats's maternal grandparents.

8f: Their son George, Yeats's uncle, was both astrologer and Mason. Yeats described his funeral in 1910 in a letter to Lady Gregory as "very touching": "The church full of the working people, Catholics who had never been in a Protestant church before . . . The Masons (there were 80 of them) had their own service and one by one threw acacia leaves into the grass with the traditional Masonic goodbye 'Alas my brother so mote it be.' " Acacia is a woody shrub.

15–16: The Mall and Eades grammar school are a street and school in Sligo.

17f: Another maternal uncle of Yeats, the sailor John Pollexfen died in Liverpool.

Title and 24f: The youngest of the Pollexfen brothers, Alfred had a rather bland personality and returned to Sligo from Liverpool in 1910 to take the place of his brother George in the family firm, W & G. T. Pollexfen and Company.

37: Yeats wrote in his autobiography that "a seabird is the omen that announces the death or danger of a Pollexfen."

UPON A DYING LADY

First published in *The Little Review*, August 1917. Yeats based the "dying lady" on Mabel Beardsley (1871–1916), sister of the artist Aubrey Beardsley, whom he had known as a young man. An avid doll collector, she was dying of cancer.

I, 8: Petronius Arbiter (AD 27–66) was a first-century Roman writer and companion of the emperor Nero.

II: The artists Edmund Dulac and Charles Ricketts brought Mabel Beardsley dolls based on drawings by her brother, Aubrey.

III, 7: Pietro Longhi (1702–85) was a Venetian genre painter.

9: Turkish trousers were cut extremely loosely.

VI, 4–6: Grania and Dermuid (more often Diarmuid) were tragic lovers in the Fenian cycle of Irish mythology; Dermuid died on the slopes of Ben Bulben. Giorgione (1478–1510) was a Venetian painter praised by Walter Pater (see note to "The Phases of the Moon," ll. 26–27) among others for his sensuous compositions.

9: Four great warriors from olden times. Achilles in *The Iliad* slew Hector, among other feats; Timor (1336–1405), better known as Tamburlaine, led the Mongol army across Asia and threatened Europe; Babar, the popular name of Zahir-ud-din-Mohammed (1483–1530), founded the Mughal empire in India; Barhaim, or Bahram Gur, was a mighty fifth-century Persian hunter and king mentioned by Edward FitzGerald in stanza seventeen of *The Rubaiyat of Omar Khayyam*.

EGO DOMINUS TUUS

First published in *Poetry* (Chicago), October 1917.

Title: "Ego Dominus Tuus" may be translated as "I am your lord." Yeats found it especially in Dante Gabriel Rossetti's translation of Dante Alighieri's *Vita Nuova*.

One of Yeats's many dialogue poems, "Ego Dominus Tuus"'s speakers' names are Latin for "this one" (Hic) and "that one" (Ille). Because of the similarity of Ille's views to Yeats's own, Yeats's friend and sometime secretary Ezra Pound quipped that the latter should have been called "Willie."

4: Michael Robartes is an invented character who appears in numerous places in Yeats's poetry and prose, including stories and the prose work *A Vision*. In a 1922 note to the poem "Michael Robartes and the Dancer," Yeats wrote of him: "Years ago I wrote three stories in which occur the names of Michael Robartes and Owen Aherne. I now consider that I used the actual names of two friends, and that one of these friends, Michael Robartes, has but lately returned from Mesopotamia, where he has partly found and partly thought out much philosophy. . . . They take their place in a phantasmagoria in which I endeavor to explain my philosophy of life and death. To some extent I wrote these poems as a text for exposition."

19: Dante Alighieri (1265–1321), author of both *Vita Nuova* and *The Divine Comedy*, among other works; they both feature his love for Beatrice.

26: Lapo Gianni (1270–1330?) and Guido Cavalcanti (1255–1300) were Italian poets and friends of Dante.

52: John Keats (1795–1821), English Romantic poet whom Yeats placed at Phase 14 of *A Vision*.

A PRAYER ON GOING INTO MY HOUSE

First published in *The Little Review*, October 1918.

1: "This tower and cottage" refer to Yeats's tower, Thoor Ballylee, with its adjoining cottage and bridge.

4: Galilee is a region in ancient Palestine, associated with the early ministry of Jesus.

10–11: "Sinbad the Sailor" is a tale in the *Arabian Nights*, which Yeats read in Sir Richard Burton's translation. On his sixth voyage, Sinbad's ship is wrecked on the shore of the Loadstone Mountain.

16: The Red Sea is an inlet of the Indian Ocean and lies between Africa and Asia. It is the scene of the Israelites' crossing under Moses in the Bible.

THE PHASES OF THE MOON

First published in *The Wild Swans at Coole* (1919). This poem reiterates some key images from earlier in the volume and looks ahead to some of those in Yeats's book of esoteric philosophy *A Vision*, first published in 1925 and revised later.

4: For "Connemara cloth," see note to line 4 of "The Fisherman."

8f: For Robartes and Aherne, see note to line 4 of "Ego Dominus Tuus."

10: The bridge and tower are presumably those of Yeats's home at Thoor Ballylee.

15: "Milton's Platonist" is the student of "Il Penseroso," who also studies philosophy in a tower.

16–17: "Shelley's visionary prince" is Prince Athanase in the eponymous poem. Percy Bysshe Shelley (1792–1822) was an important poet for Yeats, who wrote in the late essay "Prometheus Unbound" that Shelley "shaped my life." The English artist Samuel Palmer (1805–81) did an engraving called "The Lonely Tower" for an edition of Milton's shorter poems published in 1889.

26–27: English critic and writer Walter Pater (1839–

94) had an enormous influence on the "aesthetic writers" of the next generation, especially through his *The Renaissance: Studies in Art and Poetry*.

31f: In *A Vision*, Yeats divides human life into twenty-eight psychological phases according to the moon, of which two phases (phase one, of complete objectivity, and phase fifteen, of complete subjectivity) cannot sustain human life. The remainder of the poem "The Phases of the Moon" is based on those phases.

45–46: Athenae, Achilles, and Hector all appear in Homer's *Iliad*, among other places. Athenae (later Athena) was the virgin goddess of wisdom who guides the great warrior Achilles, who kills Hector, the son of the king and queen of Troy. See particularly book I, 197f., and book XXII, 330f. Friedrich Nietzsche (1844–1900) was a German philosopher who became important to Yeats after the turn of the century.

67: Mount Sinai is on the Sinai Peninsula between the Red Sea and the Mediterranean; in the book of Exodus, Moses receives the Ten Commandments there.

118: The hunchback, saint, and fool are emblems of the last three phases of the moon (twenty-six, twenty-seven, and twenty-eight). See too the second and third poems below.

THE CAT AND THE MOON

First published in *Nine Poems* (London, 1918). Minnaloushe was the name of Maud Gonne's black Persian cat. Yeats wrote the poem while staying in her house in Normandy. Yeats also used this lyric to open and close his play *The Cat and the Moon*, of which he wrote that he "allowed myself as I wrote to think of the cat as the normal man and of the moon as the opposite he seeks perpetually" (*VPl 807*).

THE SAINT AND THE HUNCHBACK

First published in *The Wild Swans at Coole* (London, 1919).

Title: In terms of *A Vision*, the hunchback (or multiple man) stands for phase twenty-six, and the saint for phase twenty-seven.

4: Starting with the first emperor, Julius Caesar (102–44 BCE), Roman emperors carried the title "Caesar."

8: A "taws" is a leather or birch whip used in punishment, particularly of schoolchildren.

10–12: Alexander the Great (356–323 BCE), king of Macedonia, conquered Greece, Egypt, and the Persian Empire. Octavian Caesar (63 BCE–AD 14) was the first emperor to succeed Julius Caesar. Alcibiades (450–404 BCE) was a Greek statesman and general who treacherously switched sides during the Peloponnesian War and the Athenian struggle against the Persian Empire.

TWO SONGS OF A FOOL

First published in *The Wild Swans at Coole* (London, 1919). In *A Vision*, the Fool is the emblem of phase twenty-eight. Some critics associate the speckled cat with Mrs. Yeats and the hare with Iseult Gonne.

ANOTHER SONG OF A FOOL

First published in *The Wild Swans at Coole* (London, 1919). Yeats associated wisdom with the butterfly earlier in the volume, where Tom O'Roughley sings that "wisdom is a butterfly / And not a gloomy bird of prey."

THE DOUBLE VISION OF MICHAEL ROBARTES

First published in *The Wild Swans at Coole* (London, 1919).

Title: Michael Robartes has appeared in the previous several poems and their notes. Here, he functions as a visionary figure.

1: The Rock of Cashel is an imposing site rearing up from the plain in County Tipperary and offering impressive 360-degree panoramic views. On the top, among other buildings, are the ruins of a chapel constructed in the early twelfth century by Cormac MacCarthy, king of Munster, which is mentioned at the end of the poem as "Cormac's ruined house."

18: In Greek art, a Sphinx usually has the head and bust of a woman and the body of a lion.

19: Siddhartha Guatama, or Buddha (563–483 BCE), was the founder of Buddhism. "Buddha" means "enlightened one." The sphinx may stand for intellect and the Buddha for emotions.

56: Homer's paragon is Helen of Troy, a recurrent symbol in Yeats's works and associated with Maud Gonne in particular.

NOTE

First published in 1919. Yeats refers to his maternal grandfather, William Pollexfen.